# Accrington Acclaimed

## Geoff Taylor & Bob Dobson

2008
Landy Publishing

ISBN: 978-1-872895-78-9

Layout by Sue Clarke
Printed by The Nayler Group Ltd., Accrington.  Tel: 01254 234247

**Landy Publishing** has also published:

**Accrington's Changing Face** by Frank Watson & Bob Dobson
**Oswaldtwistle Observed** by Mike Booth & Albert Wilkinson
**Huncoat Uncoated** by John Goddard
**Rishton Remembered** by Kathleen Broderick

Details of all currently-available titles can be obtained from:

Landy Publishing, 'Acorns' 3 Staining Rise, Staining, Blackpool, FY3 0BU
Tel/Fax: 01253 895678 (24hrs), Email: landypublishing@yahoo.co.uk

# INTRODUCTION

We have tried in the following pages to take the reader on a trip around old Accrington, which includes both Old and New Accrington, for the two were separate townships until 1878 when the new borough was incorporated. We have not restricted ourselves to the 1878 boundary, which itself was altered in 1928 when Huncoat 'came into' the borough, nor taken a ha'poth o'notice of the 1974 one. We have included visits to the suburbs - Church, Ossie, Bash, Clayton, Altham and Huncoat. Our aim has been to show pictures which have not previously been published, or at least which are not widely known, and to provide some interesting historical information alongside them. We hope that the book will interest and educate. We hope too that it will stimulate young and old to find out about Accrington's past.

On publication, we will be giving a contribution to the fund set up, with the co-operation of the 'Accrington Observer' to help reverse the temporary closure of St John's C of E church, home of the chapel dedicated to the memory of the 'Accrington Pals' because we are pals whose friendship started when we attended St John's school.

Our thanks are extended to the Accrington Local Studies Library staff, especially Linda Doody; also to Alan Parkin, John Goddard, Frank Watson, Bert Johnson, Jeff Bannister, Margaret Powell, Peter Brockbank, Kevin Gilmartin and June Huntingdon for the loan of their photographs; to Sally Watson, Helen Barrett, Cath Duckworth, Albert Wilkinson, Robert Cunliffe, Kathleen Broderick, Walter Holmes and to anyone else we have unwittingly omitted to mention for the use of their knowledge on Accrington matters.

Geoff Taylor & Bob Dobson
October 2008

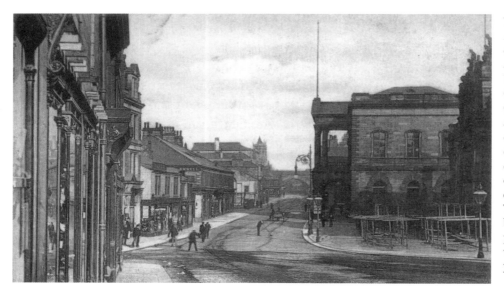

The most photographed scene in Accrington, but one which is ever-changing and full of life. We are looking down *'Little'* Blackburn Rd from just above the Commercial Hotel on the left. A Corporation man is sweeping away the evidence of horse-drawn traffic on a non-market day. The tramlines are for steam-driven trams because there are no overhead electric wires (the electric trams came in 1907). There is no *'Yorkshire Penny Bank'* building and a steam train is passing over the distant viaduct, which is only fifty years old. The year? - about 1900.

As befits its location, the Commercial Hotel was well fitted out with up-to-date facilities in 1887. It was one of the first – possibly the nineteenth - place in the town to get one of those new fangled telephones.

One of the borough's bobbies oversees a busy scene in the early years of the century. The *'Yorkshire Penny Bank'* building is in view to his left. The trams are not yet running on electric. The low buildings on his left are shops called *'Piccadilly'* and will later be knocked down to widen the road. The Town Hall stands majestic on the right, and the Market Hall is just out of view.

We are looking in the opposite direction here, but a year or two earlier. The hoardings on the right indicate that there's building going on – it's the Yorkshire Penny Bank at the corner of Blackburn Rd and St James St. It was opened in 1903. *(Photo – Jeff Bannister Collection)*

This advert was placed in 1902.

5

Accrington's architectural gems – the Market Hall and Town Hall together. It's a 1950s market day scene. The temporary (permanently so) stalls extend around the corner into Peel Street. The Market Hall's clock has been observing this scene since 1871, two years after the hall was opened.

The funeral cortege of Canon Charles Williams in 1907. He was minister for fifty years at Cannon Street Baptist church and its predecessor on Blackburn Road for fifty years. The Commercial Hotel, just out of sight to the left, closed and all its window blinds were drawn as a mark of respect to a man described as '*the best debater in the Baptist ministry*' and by the Accrington writer Richard Crossley as 'a *leader of men*'. There were three mourning carriages and a hearse, followed by private carriages then many dignitaries on foot accompanied by his congregation and fellow Baptists from across the country. Picture postcards of the procession were produced for sale.

Peel Street in 2002. The buses haven't been in the Corporation's livery since 1986. The '*outside*' market has become more permanent, though there are still changes to come. The curved pavement line in the right foreground leads into what was properly named '*Pleck Road*' and went through to Broadway. Peel Street is named after early Accrington's most important land-owning family. The Town Hall was called the '*Peel Institute*' previous to the Local Board, fore-runner of the Corporation, buying it.

On the same day the cameraman has walked into Broadway and is standing where, just a few years before, stood the Odeon cinema. There's building going on all around. To the right is an entrance to the '*Arndale*' shopping centre

It is probably true to say that Bull Bridge is the very centre of Accrington. There was a pub here in the 16th century, alongside where the river was likely to have been forded, and where the county council later built a bridge which is still visible to those traversing the roundabout which has replaced the scenes on these pages. The corner of the 'Ye Olde Black Bull' is seen on the right. In the distance on both pictures is the 3-storey building which was the Milnshaw Brewery before becoming a model common lodging house. When offered for sale in 1920, the building and its 1,200 square yards plot was advertised as 'containing a natural well'. It had the benefit of being on a 999 year leasehold from 1879, which is presumably when it was built.

The advert stated 'of interest to manufacturers, brewers, cinema proprietors'. The smaller building to the right was for many years Ward Knowles printworks. Probably as a reference to the neighbour, the company called themselves 'Model Press', though they didn't use this when in their previous premises in Clayton and Bridge Street. The firm had been founded in 1904 and vacated these premises in 1977. On the later photograph from the Accrington Library Collection, the Morris or Austin cars are outside Henry Duff's grocery shop and the 'Yankee Bar', which had formerly been the 'New Model inn' beerhouse.

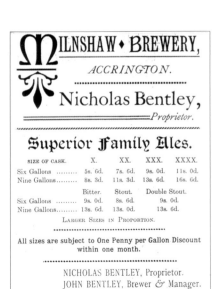

These are the 1886 prices.

Bull Bridge from the bottom of Castle Street. We see the side of the *'Black Bull'* across the river. The car is emerging from Hyndburn Rd and behind it is the fine Ambulance Drill Hall. In the earlier photo, which appears to have been taken before the Drill Hall was built in 1904, we see Mr Birtwistle's grocery shop, people crossing the bridge over the river, (then called the *'River Stink'* by locals) and the premises of John & William Whittaker. Why is Sir Henry Trickett's sign there? Perhaps there's a clue in the fact that his middle name was Whittaker. He was five times Mayor of Rawtenstall. His family had strong Accrington connections. *(Photos – Accrington Local Studies Library)*

These adverts are dated 1932. Note that *'Burne Studio'* was owned by a Whittaker.

A contingent of the Accrington Borough Police (formed in 1878, amalgamated with the county force in 1947) on what may well be a Mayor -Making Day procession. These used to be held in November, whereas now the new mayor takes over in April. The Chief Constable is not with them, as he will be at the head of the procession, or walking alongside the new mayor. A chap called Jack sent this postcard to Miss Morley of Belgrave St, Rising Bridge and wrote "I did not see you down here last Sunday", so the photograph was less than a week old.

Now in the 1960s, the Drill Hall is on the left after Taylor Street East, with Union Street on the right. Most of this photograph is now covered up by the roundabout.

The Accrington & Church Industrial Co-operative Society Ltd. played a major part in the lives of Accringtonians after its foundation in 1860. It was a force for good not only in the field of providing cheaper food, but also in culture, education and sport. In 1910 it celebrated its fiftieth birthday. Amongst the celebrations there was held a Field Day and a book was published. These gentlemen, with the two ladies, were on the *'Jubilee Committee'*.

*Back row*: M Wilkinson / Jos Pollard / H.Heyworth / Mrs Abm Shuttleworth / Geo Tilstsone / Mrs Hooley / Jas Crawford / Thomas Mayall / A Ball

*Front Row*: Wm Holmes / Jas Bradley / F.Bolitho (Sec) / Geo Brownbill (Chairman) / J J Healey / Jas Parkinson / W Eastwood.

There were various committees within the Society's framework. The ladies' ones were formed into *'guilds'*, and in 1910 they came together for this photograph.

*Back Row*: Miss Smith / Mrs Stephenson / Mrs Barlow / Mrs Mulhall / Mrs Bracewell / Miss Woods / Mrs Pickup / Mrs Lunt

*Middle Row*: Mrs Thorpe / Mrs Holey / Mrs W Haworth (Church President) / Mrs Haworth (Accrington President) / Miss D Whitemoss / Mrs Spencer / Mrs Parkinson

*Front Row*: Mrs Carter / Mrs Hindle

11

The long-awaited Co-op Field Day procession, held in July 1910.  It was *'the largest juvenile parade that ever passed though the streets of Accrington'*.

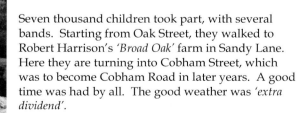

Seven thousand children took part, with several bands.  Starting from Oak Street, they walked to Robert Harrison's *'Broad Oak'* farm in Sandy Lane. Here they are turning into Cobham Street, which was to become Cobham Road in later years.  A good time was had by all.  The good weather was *'extra dividend'*.

The Co-op Field Day held in May 1905 was a grand affair. Richard Harrison, a professional photographer, took these photos. John Riley, the local president had organised it as a means of publicising the growing society and the benefits of membership. *'Several thousand well-dressed people took part'* said the Observer's reporter, telling of the *'three bands, morris and coon dancing and dumb-bell display by prettily-attired girls and boys'*. The society had 9,104 members in 1910 - to that figure should be added the members of their families.

A few of the distinctive Co-op stores (they weren't called shops) dotted throughout Accrington and Church. (Ossie had their own society): The photographer caught a visit by the society's own delivery service to the Primrose Street grocery and butcher's.

In Abbey Street the society appears to have occupied premises built before it was formed in 1860 – here are the confectionery, tailoring and outfitting departments. Further down Abbey Street were the offices and just around the corner in Oak Street were other departments, including the Assembly Rooms.

Here we see the Huncoat grocery staff in 1910 outside their recently-opened premises. It can now be seen that the society's prime movers often had a personal financial interest in what the society spent.

The society was at the forefront in education in the town, and in planning of new cotton mills which, through a building company, were leased to manufacturers. In addition, the society did some house-building.

Broadley's of Clayton was a printing business in which employees felt *"part of the family"*. Here we see the firm's cup-winning table tennis team, with their *'gaffers'*, around 1948: The firm had their own sports field off Sparth Road.

*Back Row, L-R*: Frank Lovett / Tom Hollins / Arthur Macintosh / Rex Monk / Phillip Boadley/ Arthur Sellers/ Fred Witehead

*Front Row L-R*: Phillip Broadley / Stan Fitzpatrick / Billy Smith / Harold Chippendale

A group of students from the local Technical School, which was still housed in what had just become the Grammar School building on Blackburn Rd, visiting Broadley's in July 1921. Most local employers felt the need for good relations with the college, which provided them with a skilled workforce.

The boardroom provides a meeting place for the firm's management, including the foremen of the various *'shops'*, in the late 1940s. At this time, the firm was moving away from their use of the name *'Gutenberg Works'* because of anti-German feeling in the country. They had previously been keen to align themselves with this top printing machine. The firm was started in 1841 and *'taken over'* in the late 1960s.

15

*(Right)* This scene may be in either the *'Cutting'*, *'Label Punching'* or *'Folding & Stitching'* Departments.

*(Above)* The Compositing Room: John Broadley with the foreman, Henry Wilkinson. The poster for the *'Dowry'* was being produced for Accrington's first cinema, opened four years previously. On the 1901 census, Wilkinson, is described as *'a letter press overseer'*.

*(Right)* A modern office still made use of the natural light. The calendar on the wall was supplied by Gilchrist Brothers of Leeds.

Scenes inside Broadley's works and offices in February, 1914. The scene was likely to have been similar to this since a major expansion at the works a few years previously, and would not be changed for several decades to come. For all of the firm's life, the printing of labels for food was a major part of the output. A photograph exists of a lorry laden with six and a half million labels printed for a company in South America.

A large technical workforce needed an efficient administration, with up-to date technology, such as electric light, which Broadley's produced in the works using dynamos driven by two *'gas engines'*.

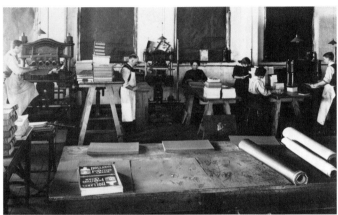

*(Left)* This was the Transferring Department, where the designs produced on stone or plate by the artist were proofed and afterwards duplicated before being passed to the printing machines. One of the men shown is Joseph Hope.

*(Right)* The ladies on this photograph include Lucy Ashton, Maggie Smith and Mabel Broadley. They are engaged in bookbinding. The firm had a large business in making account books.

*(Left)* The calendar on the wall is one produced by Broadley's. It tells us that we are looking at a scene captured in February 1914. Holland's Furniture Cream was made near Bolton. The men include foreman James Cronshaw, John James and Richard Jopson.

*(Right)* There's a Broadley's calendar on the wall. The men include George Bibby and Arthur Sellers. The staff are engaged in *'ruling'* the lines on such as account books.

17

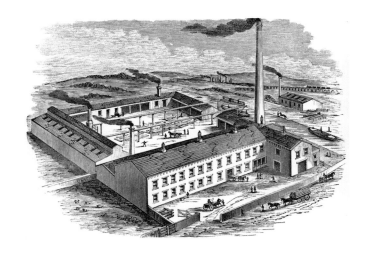

Taylor & Wilson's 'Atlas' foundry at Clayton was built 1876-7. The early directors included Henry Leach Wilson, John Clegg and William Edward Taylor. They became a limited company in 1894, producing carpet sweepers, refrigerators and heaters as well as washers and mangles. Wilson died in 1917. Taylor, who died in 1883 aged 50 years, was a fiery local politician whose brief biography in the book 'Accrington Chronology & Men of Mark' is worth reading. It is a book which should be on everyone's bookshelves.

Kevin Gilmartin took this photo in 1961 as a barge full of coal headed from Burnley to Blackburn's Whitebirk power station. Kevin, facing with his back to Church, was in a field behind Royal Mill, at the bottom of what was known locally as 'The Drive', a continuation of Read Street. The Taywil factory is on the right, with Bracewell's timber yard and sawmill on the left. Nearby is Atlas Street. Taywil's factory was called 'Atlas Works' and they made an 'Atlas' mangle.

Some items from Taywil's 1885 catalogue. They all bear the *'Phoenix'* trade mark. The company took out many patents to protect their interests. They were in competition with the *'Ewbank'*, *'Pioneer'* and Henry Slack companies. In 1919 the company advertised that they had been awarded over two hundred medals for the quality of their products. In 1942 a local 16yr old lad set fire to the building, causing damage to the value of £20,000.

The "DEXTER" CHURN.

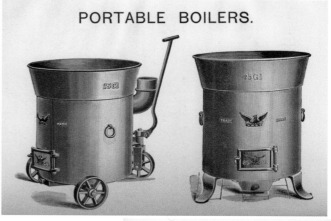

PORTABLE BOILERS.

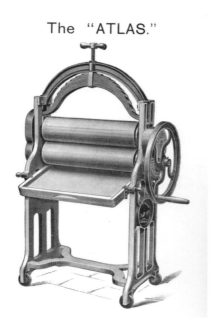

The "ATLAS."

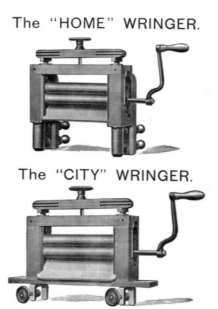

The "HOME" WRINGER.

The "CITY" WRINGER.

The "HOME" WASHER.

This postcard, postmarked 1909, calls Dill Hall Lane *'Cemetery Road'*, but it has never had this name. On an 1848 map it was *'Church Lane'*, which is the name that it assumes once it reaches Altham near to Enfield cricket ground. The present name was in use by 1892. At that time, Dill Hall farmhouse was where the petrol filling station is now. The cemetery to which the bogus street name refers is the one at the top of Dill Hall Lane and it was opened in 1889. On the card, the sender has written to Miss Nora Hartley of Colne, telling her *"this is Bertha in the doorway and her brother in law is the butcher in the butcher's shop doorway"*. Whoever Bertha was, she is at the door of No 44. The Co-op grocery and butcher's had been built since 1901. The photograph of them was taken in 1910 by the Co-op, when it operated 59 stores.

From the *'Accrington Gazette'* of 2nd April 1904.

## Correspondence.

### STREET NOISES.
#### TO THE EDITOR OF THE "GAZETTE."

Sir,—Visiting your interesting town this week, I was glad to see signs of many alterations and improvements. Last time I had occasion to put pen to paper, it was to accord my appreciation of the music provided for the people in your parks, but to-day I heard music (?) in your streets to the nature and nuisance of which I beg to draw attention. On Saturday morning I met cart after cart giving out the most hideous noises, which, I understand, comes from the application of the brake. Surely this could be remedied with a little lubrication. Many horses, I should think, would not pass the sound without a protest, and I certainly feel I cannot. Towns are noisy enough as a rule without that which could easily be removed.—Yours, etc.,

VISITOR.

---

### PEEL ATHENÆUM.
#### TO THE EDITOR OF THE PRESTON CHRONICLE.

Sir,—I read a letter some time ago, which was published in your valuable paper, desiring to know what had become of the funds which had been subscribed for the erection of this building; but no answer to the same has been made, either through the medium of your paper or in any other way. If the directors intend to satisfy the subscribers and the public, they must make known where the funds are; and whether they intend to erect such building, and when; because many inquiries are made about the same. Yours obediently,

Accrington, February 2nd, 1854. A SUBSCRIBER.

### ASSAULTS IN ACCRINGTON.
#### TO THE EDITOR OF THE PRESTON CHRONICLE.

Sir,—I take the liberty of stating, through the medium of your valuable columns, the facts of a gross outrage committed on myself, on Thursday evening last, between the hours of eleven and twelve o'clock.

As I was returning home from some business, and when near Mr. Sanderson Barnes's, Warner's Arms Inn, some person came behind me from the direction of Church-street, and gave me a dreadful blow, in consequence of which I staggered and fell down a flight of steps, and was rendered insensible, and which has incapacitated me from following my business since. A scream being set up by the occupiers, assistance was promptly at hand, and I was conveyed home by two respectable parties, who can testify to the injuries I have received.

By giving publicity in your valuable journal to the above facts it may cause our sleepy police to be a little more on the look-out to prevent such murderous attacks on persons at that hour of the night, when attending upon private transactions; and I must add that this is neither the first nor the second time I have been subjected to such cowardly and dastardly assaults.

I remain, sir, your obedient servant,

JOHN DEAN,
Accrington, Feb. 2nd, 1854. Hat Manufacturer.

---

# DESIRABLE PLOTS OF
# BUILDING LAND,
## IN ACCRINGTON.

# TO BE LET

*On reasonable Ground Rents, for terms of 999 Years,*

## SEVERAL PLOTS OF
# LAND

### In quantities to suit the requirements of persons intending to build.

The Land is very eligibly situated in the Township of Old Accrington, and recently formed part of a Close of Land called "Owens Meadow," is bounded on the northerly side by the Lancashire and Yorkshire Railway, is close to and on the Easterly side of the Turnpike Road leading out of Accrington towards Whalley, and approached from the said Road by a new Street called "Meadow Street."

---

*For an inspection of the Plan and Terms of letting application may be made to Mr. William Roberts, Builder, Park Saw Mill, Accrington; or to*

# HALL & BALDWIN,
### SOLICITORS, CLITHEROE.

*Clitheroe, 7th May, 1863.*

An Auction Notice dated 7th May 1863. This throws some light on the streets named Owen Street and Meadow Street. In 1863, some land off Castle Street near the *'Castle'* pub was described as being known as *'the Owen's tenement'*.

St Mary Magdalene's church scholars in procession up Haywood Road in the 1930s.

## Princess Garage

(RAILWAY ARCHES)

### BLACKBURN ROAD, ACCRINGTON.

Proprietor - G. NIELD.

Garage open from 9 a.m. to 12 p.m. midnight.

## REMOVING INVALIDS A SPECIALITY.

### Also TAXIS NIGHT or DAY

Distance no object.

Now opened Office on Station Stand

Telephone **2715** Accrington.

Private Address : 145 Blackburn Road, (*opposite Imperial Hotel*), Accrington.

Messages after Midnight may be left at Private Address.

A striking figure with a fine moustache, George Nield was advertising in a 1929 brochure, and was still doing so well over twenty years later. Nobody thought his advert *'politically incorrect'*.

The ladies of the New Jerusalem Church in Abbey Street turn out in their fine examples of the milliner's art on a fine day in May 1911. There's a *'converzazione'* advertised on one of the posters. This is an Italian word meaning *'concert'*. Such events were popular in church circles up to at least the 1960s. The ladies are on their way to a stone-laying ceremony at a Swedenborgian church on Fairfield Street at the corner with Spring Hill Road. Let's hope their shoes were comfortable. *(Photo- Jeff Bannister Collection)*

Bert Johnson took this photograph looking up Oak Street as the fine Congregational chapel was being demolished in 1965. It had graced Accrington's skyline since 1889 and many of the town's *'great and good'* had worshipped there. At the far side of the chapel were the various Co-op premises – grocery, clogger's. Below the chapel were shops occupied by a boot repairer, a bike shop, a hairdresser, a confectioner and a tripe dresser. Oak Street was an important shopping thoroughfare.

A roofless New Jerusalem church, also known as the *'Swedenborgian'* church, was captured by Geoff Taylor on 15th June 1987, when petrol cost £1.69 a gallon (37.3p a litre). The filling station would later become a Tesco convenience store/filling station. Times have not changed when one considers that the *'Swan Hotel'* next door had long supplied the needs of travellers along this road, a turnpike when the only horse-power had four legs.

The scholars and choir of St John's church line up – on different days possibly as it would be unusual for the girls to be on a decorated lorry on a church procession day – in the 1950s. *(Photos- Peter Brockbank)*

Building started on the church of St John the Evangelist in 1864 and it was consecrated in 1870. It is the largest in the town, with a spire which rises 128 feet. It was designed by Henry Macaulay of Accrington. A Grade 2 listed building, it contains within it a chapel dedicated to the memory of *'The Accrington Pals'*, opened in 1992 and containing the regimental drum, the Book of Remembrance and other mementoes. The *'Pals'* held their valedictory service here before marching off to war in 1915. The adjoining school has educated some of Accrington's finest (well, a couple of them anyway).

Sacred Heart R.C church and its adjacent presbytery were opened in 1869 and were to last until the early years of the present century. It took two years to build.

The *'Accrington Observer'* had a full report of the Sacred Heart procession which took place on Sunday 16th June 1912. It was the first for many years and was marshalled by John Glennan. *'Thousands turned out despite the rain which threatened to be a dampener'*. There were four bands, led by the Howard & Bullough's Band. The participants wore clothing *'from pure white to rich crimson and blue'*. Some idea of the size of the procession is obtained by knowing that there were over 28 altar bearers and over 100 children dressed in white. There were 200 members of the Guild of Children of Mary, 100 of the Sodality of St Monica, 240 of the Sodality of St Aloysius, 250 of the Sodality of St Francis Xavier and 120 of the Men's Holy Guild. The cross bearer was G Daniels. Banners were borne by Messrs Moon, Fairclough, Kelly and Singleton.

It's a time for celebrating – speeches, a band, tea and buns. The foundation stone of Whalley Road Congregational Church is being laid (Don't let the Health & Safety people see this photo). The church cost £1,600 to build in 1877 and would accommodate 400 persons. A school for 400 scholars was built next door in 1891 at a cost of about £750. *(Photo- Frank Watson Collection)*

The Cotton Street Unsectarian Church was not, as the name tells us, allied to any particular brand of Christianity. It was founded in 1888 by a group headed by the mayoress, Mrs Williamson Lee, and prided itself that it took in the town's *'ragged children'*. The initial cost of the building was £700. For many years it was customary that new mayors would attend evening service here on Mayor's Day.

The 1936 centenary booklet for Green Haworth chapel opens with *'Green Haworth, reached by a long ascent, stands on top of a bleak, windswept hill. A century ago, this was known as a wild, outlandish place; it was a rendezvous for a number of abandoned fellows whose ruffian exploits were a terror to the neighbourhood.'* Methodist missionaries to Green Haworth were sent from Union Street chapel in 1809. In 1836 there were 24 members, and congregations averaged one hundred, though the building would hold five hundred. At the centenary celebrations, one of the visiting ministers was Rev. Jimmy Butterworth, a local lad whose name will be forever honoured by Ossie folk. In 1948, the first marriage ceremony took place there, and it closed with a final service in 1985, having been bought by a local farmer.

1907 was a very busy year for Spring Hill Methodists. In March the new Sunday school was opened. A procession walked from the old to the new school building for a 3pm ceremony. The old building had been sold for £4,000 to the Corporation for school building and the new ones (church and school) cost another £6,000 on top of that figure. Of a grand design by Accrington architects Grimshaw & Cunliffe, it had ten classrooms and a hall which could accommodate six hundred. The Infants Department had four classrooms to accommodate two hundred scholars. The opening was *"favoured by good weather"*.

The new chapel was opened in September. The President of the Wesleyan Conference was the main preacher over the weekend, though at the Children's Service, the mayor, Mr Higham, played the organ. At the evening meeting, the electric lights kept going out. No doubt the gathering blamed *'modern technology'*.

This is believed to be a group of Spring Hill Methodist ladies intent on fund-raising in the early days of the century, when a new church and school were being planned. The pictures behind them have a Boer War look about them.

These are photographs of two church processions in Church. Which church or churches we don't know. They were taken just a few yards apart, on Blackburn Road between Ernest Street and Henry Street and possibly on the same day. An adjacent street is given the name *'Edward'* and there are several other streets in Church given Christian names.

How convenient it is when a photographer has taken the trouble to write on his photographs not only the event but also the date. There was no mention of this *'Olde Englishe Concert'* in the *'Accrington Observer'* in 1912. Just imagine the laughs these lasses had. In the paper's edition of 4th July 1914 there was an advert placed by the Antley Methodists. It was to do with the 50th Anniversary Jubilee Reunion and *'re-opening of the chapel after beautifying'*.

When the stones were officially laid at St Andrew's church, Swiss Street, on Saturday May 12th, 1912, it was a time for celebrating. It was Whitsuntide weekend and all the church scholars of the town, bodies such as the freemasons and other

organisations joined in. Lord Derby, on behalf of the freemasons, had laid a corner stone the previous Thursday. There were thousands of children and grown ups in the procession and the weather was fine. Here we see the St James', Church Kirk contingent on their way. Canon Rogers from St James' church, Accrington, was one of the stone-layers along with the vicar of St Andrew's, Rev. Spencer. (Wondering why there are two churches so close together with the same name?) The happy event concluded with the singing of the national anthem and that fine hymn *'All People That On Earth Do Dwell'*. The stone building had replaced an earlier *'tin tabernacle'*.

George Croft was landlord at the Hargreaves Arms, Manchester Road about 1910. Which of these chaps is George? Is that Mrs Croft? The pub had been in operation for about eighty years by then. It was the scene of great celebration on Queen Victoria's coronation day in 1838. At 9am, a procession headed by the coach *'Rocket'* drawn by four horses, was followed by Sunday school scholars, members of Friendly Societies and the principal inhabitants of Old and New Accrington. A field day was held, and the inns of the town(s) provided roast beef, plum pudding, ale and a glass of spirit with which to drink Her Majesty's health. Ninety gentlemen sat down in the Hargreaves Arms, presided over by Benjamin Hargreaves, after whose land-owning family the hotel was named. Fireworks concluded the events of the day.

Nuttall's was a Blackburn-based brewery formed in 1894. The company owned 105 'pubs. It became part of the Matthew Brown company, makers of *'Lion'* ales, in 1927. *(Photo- Jeff Bannister Collection)*

The *'Bee Hive'* was a beerhouse (i.e. it didn't sell spirits) in Bank Street at the corner of Oak Street, close by the *'Abbey Hotel'*. Nathaniel Berry was the landlord in 1909. At this time on Bank Street there were also the *'Clogger's Arms'* and the *'Farrier's Arms'*, with others in adjacent streets. There was also a *'Bee Hive Inn'* on Manchester Road, Baxenden.

The *'Horse Shoe'* beerhouse was at the junction of Crawshaw Street and School Street. In this 1950s photograph, complete with a Hillman Husky van, we can see that a doorway has been bricked up. Why was it so called? It was common for breweries to give 'pubs names which had a horse-racing connection, but it may be too that this was a reference to the farrier's workshop at the other end of Crawshaw Street. There was also a smithy in nearby King Street before the Ambulance Brigade Hall was opened in 1904. Towards the end of its life, in the 1960s, the Horse Shoe had the reputation of being a *'little lads' pub'*, i.e. one where lads under 18yrs of age could get a drink illegally.

On 7th December 1939 a letter written the previous day arrived at the Accrington Police Office. It was written *'in a good hand'* in ink:-

> Dear Sir, How is it that the Oddfellows Home and Welcome Inn can keep open all day to about one o'clock in the morning selling drink. It is no wonder they can go up and down boasting what drink they can sell especially Friday afternoon & Saturday with plenty of women in. They are now selling pool tickets for Christmas. You must excuse me but there is some of your own lot what informs them when there is something going to be done.

It was not signed. Who wrote it? Perhaps a woman whose husband was one of the customers, perhaps a disgruntled law-abiding licensed victualler. Certainly a resident near to the two 'pubs, which were in Blackburn Road and Elephant Street respectively. The officer receiving the letter marked it *'For attention'*.

The Baxenden Working Men's Club was in Hill Street at the Manchester Road end of the block on the right. It closed about 1956. After a spell as a joiner's workshop where coffins were made, it became part of the house next door. The room upstairs in this 1930s (?) photograph was the concert room. Part of the mechanism for lowering barrels into the cellar can still be seen attached to the wall, as well as part of the sign. At one time, in addition to this club, there was a Conservative Club (which is still active) and the Gladstone Liberal Club which was on Manchester Road close to Rock Street. And then there were the 'pubs.

Arthur Mortimer was a *'character'*; here we see him outside Geoff Taylor's butcher's shop in Plantation Street in the 1980s. Arthur was daft on steam traction engines and fairground organs. He was a mate of the Bolton steeplejack Fred Dibnah, and was like him in many ways – his oily flat cap is testament to that. Very keen on his smallholding, he had been gardener to Miss Grimshaw of Owl Hall for some years. On the wall behind him is a letter-box which has been there since Queen Victoria's days.

This is James Albert Taylor, who was born at in 1897, so this photo of him as a teenager would be taken just before the Great War in the family's back yard in Hillock Vale. Diminutive in stature, James tells us something about lads of that time in that they dressed in the style of their fathers – clogs, cap, waistcoat (which he would call his 'weskit') and a large coloured neckerchief tied around his neck as a tie. The clogs and his whippet made young James an archetypal Lancashire lad. (What's bettin' he smoked Woodbines and Park Drive?)

There was no better ice-cream than Birtwell's, (unless it was Trickett's), which was made up Huncoat. The cart is in Ramsbottom Street, with Haywood Road behind it. The photographer is unknown, but it was taken about 1958 going off the dress style of the girl customer in white ankle socks and a full, circular skirt showing a bit of underskirt. She probably had a black elasticated *'waspie'* with a big *'silver'* buckle around her waist. She probably had a *'pony-tail'* too. By this time there were motorised ice-cream vans, so this is towards the end of a horse-drawn era. Just out of the cameraman's range there would be a chap with a bucket and shovel waiting to scoop up anything that the horse left to put on his garden. *(Photo –Alan Parkin Collection)*

What a picnic today's Environmental Health people would have with this man. As he is outside the shop of Milton Gregson, No 4 Eddleston Street, a *'fruiterer and greengrocer'*, we can be fairly sure that he is hawking those products around Spring Hill and beyond. It may well be that this is Mr Gregson, complete with muffler, *'brat'* and clogs. The wheels on his cart never got punctures. The wheel on the front of his cart is a device to help with braking. Next door at No 2 is the Spring Hill Post Office, which had several homes. By the 1930s, this shop was a baker's. *(Photo- Alan Parkin Collection)*

No motor cars in view as we look down Lonsdale Street. The Spring Hill Working Men's Club, the fine building on the left, was granted a *'club certificate'* to supply intoxicants in January 1907, and this photograph is of that time. In the distance is the railway bridge. On the right is a shop at the corner of Charter Street which would become a Post Office kept by the dignified, laugh-loving Fred Hindle, a prisoner of war in Burma who returned home not having slept in a bed for six years. He had no great fondness for the Japanese.

33

The Nayler name has been associated with printing in the area since 1920, when the firm was started. For many years it was based in Union Road, Ossie, and here we see the premises in the background behind the works outing about to set off on the 1951 Festival of Britain celebration trip. The building to the right had been acquired as an extension and the roof light added to give daylight for the workforce, some of whom we see here under that window. The then managing director, Eric Nayler, son of the founder is standing on the right against the coach. His son John took over the reins and has passed them to his son, Alastair. In 1956 the firm moved into Aero Mill, Edward Street, Church. Other printing businesses have since been acquired and they now trade as 'The Nayler Group'.

Also shown is a letter-heading from their Union Road days. The Burnley telephone number was that of the family home.

BOOKBINDING · STATIONERY · OFFICE REQUISITES

# NAYLER
## The PRINTER

TELEPHONE
ACCRINGTON
2752

TELEPHONE
BURNLEY
3658

OSWALDTWISTLE
LANCS.

Who are these lads?  Are they at work or play?  We don't know, but we can be pretty certain that they are local lads, as Mr Winkfield of 51 Rhyddings Street, Ossie took their photograph and put his stamp on it.  It has the look of around the First World War about it, so maybe these lads were not old enough to join up.  Mr Winkfield's stamp was of the rubber type, suggesting that he wasn't fully professional.  He doesn't appear in any directories or in the 1901 census, but in 1909 there was a firm called Southworth & Sons in business in Rhyddings Street.  However, it gives us a chance to observe their dress style.

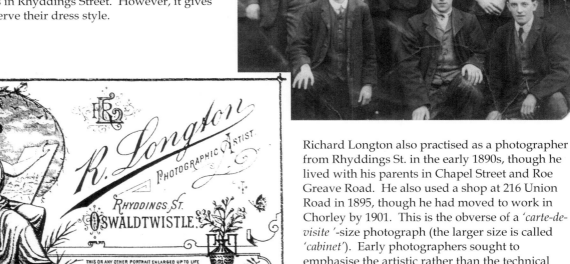

Richard Longton also practised as a photographer from Rhyddings St. in the early 1890s, though he lived with his parents in Chapel Street and Roe Greave Road.  He also used a shop at 216 Union Road in 1895, though he had moved to work in Chorley by 1901.  This is the obverse of a 'carte-de-visite'-size photograph (the larger size is called 'cabinet').  Early photographers sought to emphasise the artistic rather than the technical aspect of their work and saw themselves as successors to artists who painted and drew their subjects.

Frenchman Frederick Steiner was an industrial chemist whose great works put Church on the map.  This is a heading from the company's notepaper.

35

It has been said with justification that Saturday 11th June 1904 was *'the biggest day in Accrington's history'*. The *'Hero of Mafeking'*, Major-General Baden-Powell came to town to open the new St John's Ambulance Drill Hall on Bull Bridge. He was met at the railway station by Mr Bolton of Highbrake House, Huncoat and taken in a carriage to the Town Hall, where he was presented with an illuminated address. The afternoon procession is what made this an unforgettable day. The majority of the town's 100,000 population turned out to see the three thousand who took part in it, including 900 St John's members from all over the country, 800 men of the local regiments, over 200 Boys' Brigade members, firemen, mounted police, seven band including Accrington's own Pipe Band, and the Chief Constable with a posse of mounted police. They moved from Avenue Parade along Blackburn Road to the *'new'* Technical School (later the Grammar School) then returned to the Drill Hall. 'B-P' is the man with much braid on his hat.

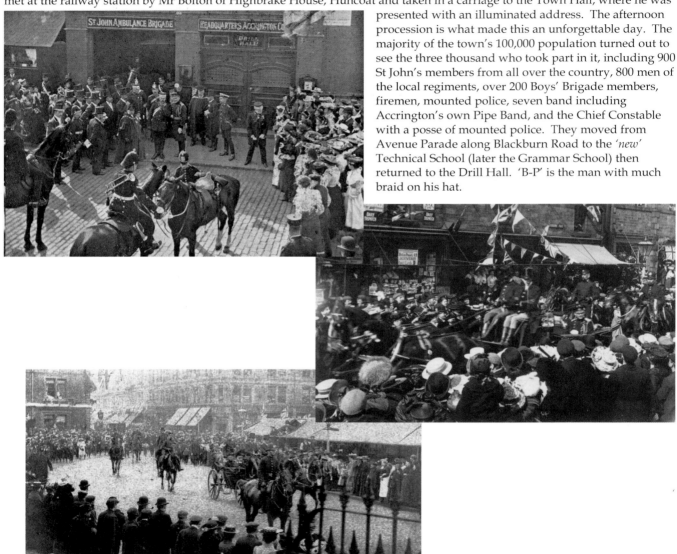

A scene inside the new Drill Hall captured by J W Tattersall, a prominent Accrington photographer. The Ambulance movement had begun in Accrington in 1884 in a room behind the Fire Station near the Market Hall before moving to two lots of premises in Bridge Street and then, in 1898 to the Bull Bridge site. In four years, they moved into the new Drill Hall. At this time, the *'Accrington Corps'* was driven by Thomas Whittaker, supported by his family. They may well have owned land in the Bull Bridge area.

### St. John Ambulance Brigade.—No. 4 District.

### Accrington Corps. Bull

Please address all communications to Head Quarters.

Head Quarters, BRIDGE,
ACCRINGTON.

The Clerk to the Urban District
Council of Church.

May 26th 1904.

Dear Sir,

Major General Baden Powell C.B. opens our New Drill Hall on Saturday June 11th. The Officers of the Corps have asked the Corporation of Accrington to give the occasion official recognition, and we should be pleased to have the cooperation of your Council.

So far as the work of the Accrington Corps St John Ambulance Brigade is concerned, the whole district is on the same footing as regards first aid appliances and free horse ambulance service.

Yours faithfully,
Ogden
Chief Supt.

In 1904 the Corps had a strength of 85, arranged as officers, sergeants, corporals and privates. They owned a horse-drawn ambulance wagon, a litter, 17 stretchers, and various equipment such as crutches. They maintained 17 first aid boxes on the streets and placed 72 haversacks in the town's mills.

The Brigade had not changed its headed notepaper since moving to Bull Bridge a few years previous to when this letter was sent by Chief Superintendent Ogden, who lived at 157 Whalley Road, to Church UDC.

The Accrington Municipal Technical School started life in 1895, and this picture would be taken soon after that. Costing £13,000, it was designed by Accrington architect Henry Ross. In 1906, it was enlarged by the addition of two side wings at a cost of £8,000, and in 1921 its name was changed to *'Accrington Grammar School'*. For some years, it housed pupils (of both sexes) of both the Grammar School, the Technical School and the School of Arts & Crafts. In 1939, the girls moved to the new High School at Moorhead. The cramped conditions were realised at an early stage, but it was not until 1968 that the boys moved to a new school, also at Moorhead. In the Blackburn Road years, nearly 8,000 pupils had been on the register, taught by 225 members of staff under five headmasters. In 1975, political dogma brought about the end of this and many other grammar schools.

In 1998, the old school was demolished to make way for housing, but in 2008 a blue plaque was put up on a wall there by the Accrington Grammar School Old Boys Association to commemorate a fine institution.

The Grammar School prefects in July, 1938.
*(Photos–Margaret Powell)*
Boys:
1–Sagar, 2–Hammond, 3-Walker, 4-Westall, 5-Dalton, 6-Sutcliffe, 7-Hargreaves, 8-Haworth, 9-Bullock, 10-Macgregor
Girls:
1-Kathleen Barnes, 2-Joan Brown, 3-May Wilkinson, 4-Cathie Holmes, 5-Olive Wetherall, 6-Marion Littlefair, 7-Ruth Hayes, 8-Jeanne Stansfield, 9-Margaret Barton, 10-Gladys Parkinson, 11-Ethel Haworth, 12-Doris Haworth

*"Let's be off and enjoying ourselves"* is what these regulars at the *'Hope & Anchor'* in Whalley Road are saying as they pose outside the 'pub before setting in a *'chara'* for Blackpool in 1957. No doubt the boot would be loaded down with crates of ale to slake throats made dry with all that singing and laughing.

Radio and TV personality Barbara Kelly, no doubt accompanied by her husband Bernard Braden, laughs with Peggy Watson and Edna Taylor when she visited the Burco Dean factory in Lupin Road in the early 60s. The firm made washing machines and boilers. Perhaps there was an edition of a programme such as *'Workers' Playtime'* being planned. Three rum lasses together.

From an earlier period, perhaps the 1920s or 30s, an advert placed in the *'Accrington Observer'* by hairdresser Tom Pateman. Tom was the author of *'Dunshaw; a Lancashire Background '*, published in 1948. It is about life in *'Dunshaw'*, which is in fact Accrington - highly recommended.

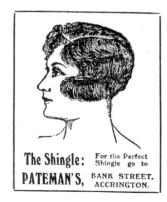

39

These two photographs show the family of Dr Gordon Hanna, who lived at *'Pleck House'*. They were taken before 1910, when Dr Hanna was sentenced to five years imprisonment for performing an illegal operation and had his name removed from the Medical Register. It was later knocked down and replaced by the shop premises called *'Steinway House'*, at the corner of Whalley Road and Broadway, (formerly called *'Marquis Street'*). However, as the 1949 advert tells us, that was not the end of his medical career. An earlier occupant had been Thomas Marquis, whose name was commemorated in the street alongside his extensive house. *(Photos – Frank Watson Collection)*

40

'Pleck' is a word of Scandinavian (?) origin meaning 'place'. There was a 'Pleck Brook' running down what is now Peel Street from Avenue Parade, and the short street between Peel Street and Broadway was 'Pleck Road', sometimes called 'Pleck Back'. It is shown on this photograph, taken in the early 1960s. Probably the old building on the right is that used by Mr Duckworth, who advertised his business and his home address, perhaps because he didn't have a telephone. The Odeon cinema building is seen in the distance, and the tall building at the end belonged to Messrs Lamb, wholesale fruit merchants. Kenyon Street, which ran off Whalley Road down to Bull Bridge, was also called 't'Pleck' by locals. (Photo- Accrington Local Studies Library)

Here we see some Corporation workmen at work in 1937 where Pleck Brook joined the River Hyndburn alongside Pleck Road. The wooden hoardings are in Broadway. Later, the brickwork would be heightened to totally culvert the river.

41

The pupils of the Baptist Day School on Willow Street. It had been built in 1864 to meet what the Blackburn Road Baptists, who had acquired land around Cannon Street for a new church, perceived as a need to educate children along Christian lines.

This photograph of a mixed-sexes class shows them with the head teacher, Alonzo Langham, who had arrived in 1872 and who stayed for thirty years, which is as long as the school lasted. In the Sunday school classes, the sexes were divided. There's another clue as to this being a day school rather than a Sunday school group – the children are scruffier than they would have been in their Sunday clothes.

Here we see an older Alonzo Langham with his family, probably taken just before he died, aged 78yrs in 1930. In addition to the active part he played in the life of Cannon Street Baptists church, he had been a magistrate, a councillor, secretary of the Mechanics' Institute and treasurer of Victoria Hospital. His best work was that in connection with the new schools – Peel Park, Woodnook and Hyndburn Park. Without them, our town would be a much poorer place. *(Photo- John Goddard Collection)*

The pupils of St John's Infants School about 1950, with their teachers Miss Edna Riley, on the left, and Miss Grace Salthouse on the right. Miss Salthouse was head of the Infants School and sister–in-law of the headmaster, Harry Place, who was known to his pupils as *'Fluke'*. They each had a long association with both school and church. To encourage competition, the school was divided up into houses:- *'Beavers, Otters, Squirrels and Wolves'*.

Miss Riley's class of 1948. She came to St John's from college in 1941 and stayed a mere forty years. She taught both of the compilers of this book. Since retiring, she has (we write in the present tense) continued her association with, and interest in, the church and school. Generations of Accrington lads and lasses have her and her colleagues to thank for their abilities with the *'three R's'* and for the grounding given them in education.

A group of cup-winners who represented St John's at the annual inter-schools Sports Day usually held on Highams' Playing Fields. The photo was taken in the pocket-handkerchief-size school yard in 1954. Note that their *'pumps'* were not uniform in colour; some white, some black, maybe some brown.

Back Row, L-R: C Craig /C Downes/ K Hope/ P Fenton
Middle Row: J Loftus / P Arthur/ E Brockbank/ L Scott/ B Cotton/ R Hoyle
Front Row: A Loftus / H Downes

Hyndburn Park Council School came about, along with its sisters at Peel Park, Woodnook and Spring Hill, in the same period of hectic activity following an Education Act which required local authorities to educate their young and empowered them to build. It was opened to the public to inspect for a few days before the official opening on Friday 17th August 1906. 'An Observer Man' took advantage of this and was not greatly impressed by the interior, though he said of the exterior *"There is not an elementary school superior to this, or even equal to it"*. The Technical (later Grammar) School had been open just eleven years, but already the Education Committee had realised that more room was needed in their schools – Hyndburn Park got it. Nineteen months under construction, the new school replaced those at Union Street and Antley Methodist churches. It had thirteen classrooms each capable of holding up to sixty pupils. At the time of opening, Accrington had over 7,000 pupils and 200 teachers, not all of whom were *'certificated'*.

Mayor Nuttall opened Peel Park School on Wednesday 24th August 1910 with a gold key. It was the fifth council school since the 1903 Elementary Education Act came into operation in the borough. It was designed by Mr Newton, the Borough Engineer, (Newton Drive is named after him) at an estimated cost of £17,000. Figures for the cost of the other schools were given:- Hyndburn Park £17,480; Spring Hill £4,726; Hannah Street £1,800; Woodnook £14,273.

The staff of Spring Hill Council School about 1945. Headmaster Harry Barton is on the back row at the left. *(Photo- Margaret Powell)*

In a 1910 by-election, Liberal Harold Trevor Baker, a barrister from Sawley, beat the Conservative candidate by 2,500 votes. When one reads the 'Accrington Observers' of the time, it seems not surprising, for the editor was clearly in the Baker camp. He won too at the general election later in the year and was to remain Accrington's MP until 1918. There were no elections in the Great War, when Baker served in various important positions in the War Office. However, he was ousted in 1918, in which election the electorate had increased from 15,000 to almost double that figure. This was because women had been given the vote. All men had too, and the Accrington constituency had been increased to take in Church, Ossie, Huncoat and Altham.

**ACCRINGTON DIVISION**
## PARLIAMENTARY ELECTION,
1910.

DON'T let them Tax Daddy's Dinner.
# Vote for Baker
*Printed and Published by Jas. Broadley Ltd., Accrington.*

Probably taken just before the Great War, this photograph shows young Francis Geoffrey Macalpine, son of Sir George, being driven in a carriage by coachman Mr Day out of the family home, *'Broad Oak House'*. He would soon be with the *'Accrington Pals'* in the Somme, winning a Military Cross before coming home to resume life as director of local brick and chemical companies. He was chairman of the magisterial bench when he died in 1957. Although his parents and brother were ardent Baptists, Francis aligned himself to St Paul's church. *(Photo – Frank Watson Collection)*

Although they had cause to be proud, having beaten all challengers to win the *'Knock-out Cup'* in 1923, the achievement of the Clayton Church Institute footballers didn't make the sports pages in the *'Accrington Observer'*.

In 1910, when St John's won the *'Sir George Bullough Challenge Cup'* against opposition from teams in the local league, most churches had teams to represent them at sports. The vicar and the church elders share the team's pride. The cup appears to have *'got lost'* after 1931.

St Johns C.C. Winners of the Sir George Bullough Challenge Cup 1910

How much would a pair of these *'pads'* bring on eBay? This photograph was taken by local chap Mr Platt in Garfield Street, just behind St Paul's church.

In footballing circles there have been 3 famous teams from Accrington: a) Accrington FC who were amongst the original teams in the Football League, b) Accrington Stanley, whose name is known throughout the world and c) Bell's Temperance.

Here we see a Stanley team, possibly that which played the opening game of the 1924 season at home in front of 7,496 spectators. The manager is Sam Pilkington and the *'goalie'* Ernie Salt. The photographer, Richard Hughes, lived at 64 Burnley Rd.

About 1883 William Bell, a temperance missionary, visited Accrington. He so impressed a group of young chaps that they decided to start a club on *'total abstinence'* principles. They called it *'Bell's Temperance Working Men's Club'* and it was in Cotton Street. Within weeks they moved to rooms in Nuttall Street, and in a few more months they had so many members that they set about buying a place of their own in Belfield Rd, then called Robert Nuttall Street. A football team was started and entered in the Lancashire Junior League. They were twice winners of the cup. The photo shows the 1885-6 season cup-winning team. All would be local lads. The field they played on became known as *'Bell's Field'*. The club remained a force for good in the town for many years.

(L-R)  A Tattersall (Sec) / A Warburton / JH Whittam / W Renshaw / H Parkinson / J Watson/ L Pemberton/ EJ Holden (Chairman) JR Swindlehurst (captain) / J Heaton/ L Clarkson
G Law/ G Entwistle/ E Holgate/ Richard Sproule

Detective work has enabled us to learn Sproule's Christian name. On the photograph as originally published, only his surname was printed, but we now know that it was Richard. What were his views on temperance in view of the fact that his father was a grocer and beerseller in Royds Street?

47

A 3-nil win for the St John's lads, captained by Harold Secker, but this was after two matches and twenty minutes of extra time to find a winner of the Mayor's Cup had ended in a draw. Holy Trinity were the reigning champions, having won the cup in the previous three seasons and had been finalists each year the cup had been played for. When Mayor Bury in his speech mentioned this, someone in the crowd (the *'Observer'* reported) shouted out, *"Aye, that's wod Accrington corn'd do".* All the winners received a gold medal, including a lad called Batty who had played in the previous drawn matches but was dropped for this match.
*'Later in the evening, the St John's team drove around in a char-a-banc, proudly displaying the trophy they had won.'*

Richard Harrison put his name on this photograph, but not the date, which was June 1905. *'We have suffered'* may have referred to the Church players who had allowed Accrington's Tom Flowers to take six wickets for 19 runs. The custom of whitewashing at the Accrington/Church boundary started in 1892 and finished in 1975. Between 1974 and 1978, when local lad Alan Worsick was Accrington's *'pro'* and performed well in a derby match, the mark, painted under cover of darkness, read *'Church Wor Sick'*. After a 1913 match, neighbouring Enfield's gate receipts amounted to £8. They campaigned for an away fixture on future derby days. Huge crowds attended these matches.

Quite who these youngsters are we don't know, but they were the winners of *'The Granville Slack Shield'* which was presented to them by the *'Accrington Schools Sports Association'* in 1935.

If ever a chap deserved to be called an *'Accrington Man of Mark'*, it was Robert *'Bob'* Rush, who died in tragic circumstances in 2007 aged 94yrs. An Accrington Grammar School lad, he became a pharmacist with an abiding interest in public transport. His knowledge of Accrington's bus and trams system was encyclopaedic. He wrote two books on the subject, one on the East Lancashire railway and others in his field, illustrating them with his detailed drawings. A former organist and teacher at Cambridge St Methodist chapel, he was a gentle man and a gentleman.

John Richardson was born at Church in 1895 and died in Accrington in 1957. He played for *'t' Stanley'* both before and after they entered the Football League in 1921. Before that, he had been a sergeant in the Howitzer Brigade, and was decorated with a Military Medal.

David Richardson is the area's only FIFA-level referee. Born into a sporting family in 1937, he took up refereeing locally in 1959, moving up the levels to Football League and then FIFA standard. Amongst his *'big matches'* are the 1980 League Cup final and the 1979 FA Trophy final. In 1982, he *'ran the line'* in the European Cup final. Having had the whistle blown on him, he keeps in touch through his activities with the Lancashire F.A. and the East Lancashire Football Alliance, which runs junior football for several thousand youngsters.

Who is the Accrington man most *'looked up to'*? Forget Peel, Hargreaves, Bullough or Haworth – that man is Richard Hacking, for it was he who had charge of the building of the 21 magnificent arches carrying the new (in 1847) railway over the town. **'RH'** had his initials carved in a keystone of one of the arches, there to remain for ever as a monument to him, his craftsmen and the stone from our local quarries.

Stand in King Street with your back to Church and you'll see him – if you look up.

Three 1920s pictures from a family album. The McMyns were a well-to-do and well-connected family. They lived at 4, Holly Bank, (which is now 54 Hollins Lane) and at *'Oak Leigh'* in Manchester Road (now 241) and owned, during the Great War, a chemical company at Baxenden whose main product was new on the market - saccharin. One of their connections was with the Lightbowns, makers of toffee, who bought *'Oak Leigh'* from them. They lived in Accrington from 1916 and had gone by 1928. Here we see them in their Hollins Lane garden with friends or family and on, perhaps, another day which wasn't as hot, when the men :- JR McMyn, R Brockshaw, S Brockshaw and A Lenthall – played bowls. These were not local men.

After some years in which there had been a desire amongst the town's elders to establish a public library, and some in which a library of sorts had been operated by the Mechanics' Institute, on Saturday 18th January 1908, Accrington Public Library was opened by Mayor Higham using a golden key. It would not have come about so early without a generous donation from Andrew Carnegie, the steel magnate whose benevolence to education in this country is still paying dividends. The building was designed by William Newton, the Borough Engineer and cost £10,000. The *'Accrington Observer'* went to town on describing the fittings and facilities …. a staircase of Warmden stone; a lecture room to accommodate 500 persons (it is restricted to 90 today). Perhaps the greatest benefit was the provision of electricity, with *'switchboards'* (switches?) on both floors. The side on Willow Street was left as brick in anticipation of an extension (This came about later when the Children's Library was opened). The mayor said that this was the greatest municipal event in his mayoralty, *'one calculated to increase the happiness, learning and goodness of everyone who would take advantage of the open doors of the Free Library'*. Being *'free'* was seen as a great boon, as this was a new concept in British life which had been promoted in Accrington since 1875.

The Borough Reference Library's bookplate shown here is based upon the design of the magnificent stained glass window which is seen when ascending the library's stairs. It contains several memorable phrases, amongst them that great truism – *'Knowledge is Power'*.

A centenary celebration was held in the library on 18th January 2008. A brass band played, there were speeches by town, county and library officials. Librarian Cath Duckworth gave a resume of the years leading up to this fine building's birthday.

A lady risks getting run over as she walks towards the *'Hyndburn Bridge Hotel'* in 1907, perhaps in order to get a better view of the train passing over the distant bridge on the line known as *'the Harwood loop'*. The pub was opened in 1894, the railway in 1876. *(Photo- Frank Watson Collection)*

Enfield Soap Works had the double advantage of being alongside both the canal and the main road at Clayton. Built in 1844 by James Hacking and his associates, it was the headquarters of the *'East Lancashire Soap Company'*, whose most famous product was *'Dr. Lovelace's'* soap, and in particular their *'floating'* soap. (It floated because of the amount of oil in it.) The company operated until 1959, after which the site, seen here in the early years of the century when horses provided the horse-power, ran down and demolition followed. *(Photo – Alan Parkin Collection)*

The 'Altham Colliery Company' was in existence before 1824. Deep mining was undertaken in Altham and Clayton and Huncoat, and the Altham companies became active in the processing of coal into by-products in the 1920s. These photographs give an indication of the pit-top activities undertaken once the coal had reached the surface. They were probably taken before the National Coal Board took over all pits in 1948 at which time 'Altham Collieries' were owned by the Macalpine family. The railway line shown ran from their Moorfield site into Huncoat colliery, which was linked to the main rail system.

Altham Colliery Company owned several pits and used several means of transport to distribute their products, including this fodder eater, seen here with the chap who had to pick up any coal which had fallen off the cart. The photograph was taken about 1908.

David Nuttall was in business as a grocer at 115, Abbey Street in 1897. By 1909, 115 had become what we will call a *'chip shop'*. Behind this property was *'Briggs Yard'* which contained seven cramped dwellings. Entry to the yard is through the archway. When the photograph was taken, about 1900, the first electricity cables were being laid in Abbey Street. *(Photo- Alan Parkin Collection)*

Directly across the road from Nuttall's shop was this block at the top of Black Abbey St. On the corner is Mr Green's grocery shop, which appears to have closed down. Next door at *'Albion House'*, Obadiah Shields is a licensed game dealer and fishmonger. *(Photo- Accrington Local Studies Library)*

Sydney Street had his green grocer's shop in Washington Street in the 1930s. He had a good source for supplying rabbits. There is no shop in today's Accrington with as many rabbits in stock.

Poland Street is just out of view on the right, then there's Holland Street, and Sacred Heart RC church is further along. One of the pair standing outside the Blackburn Rd shop will be James Baron, cycle and oil dealer, hence the metal *'BP'* sign. At the other end of the block is a butcher's shop. We cannot see any overhead electric tram wires, so the photo was taken whilst the *'cars'* were steam-driven, i.e. before 1907. *(Photo – Alan Parkin Collection)*

BLACKBURN Rᵈ, ACCRINGTON. Nº5.

The only traffic seen in this photograph taken in the early years of the century by A. F. Sergeant is the passenger train pulled by an *'L & Y'* (Lancashire & Yorkshire) engine over the viaduct, which was then just over fifty years old. On a board over his King Street shop, just beyond the *'Cattle Market'* 'pub, Mr Waddington is advertising his undertaking and floristry businesses. The metal sign hanging on the left is above one of Mr Smith's three clog shops. This shop was still there in the 1950s. The lads on the left are walking past the *'Spread Eagle'* 'pub. *(Photo - Frank Watson Collection)*

55

This Abbey Street shop is seen around 1900, when Herr von Buelow was in the news. The chap in the wheelchair may have lost his legs in the Boer War. *'Sixsmith's Timetable'* gave details of East Lancashire Railway trains and was published by Broadley's of Clayton. The shop was close by Wesley Methodist church and would have a good sale for the religious matter advertised in its window. It could well be the shop, opposite the New Jerusalem church, occupied in 1910 by Mr Bartram. The lads are sat on the wooden planks which, when taken up, allowed entry to the shop's cellar. *(Photo- Alan Parkin Collection)*

This shop in Bank Street, at the corner of Infant Street, appears to be empty. In the 1890s it was occupied by George Haworth, a *'music professor'*, who may well have left when Donald Munroe *'snapped'* it. He was engaged as a photographer at various addresses between 1894 and 1925. Oh that we could see his stock of slides, plates and negatives. *(Photo- Frank Watson Collection)*

We are looking up Dowry Street with St John's church on the skyline. At the left foreground is the Co-op shop shown on the other photograph. It is likely that the *'Dowry'* refers to some land involved in a family, perhaps the Peel family, wealth settlement. Whittaker's ironworks, where the horse and cart are, was founded here in 1854, and the shop was built, with 4 houses alongside it in Dowry Street, in 1869 at a cost of £1,387. There are three Co-op departments here; grocery, butchery and clogging, though later only the grocery remained. A telephone was installed in all of the local Co-op shops in 1885. The photographer is standing in Moore Street, and just on his right was a factory, originally run by Peter Pilkington, which was converted into Accrington's first cinema, *'The Dowry'* in 1910.

The 5-digit telephone number indicates that this is a letter-heading from the 1960s, when the firm, makers of *'New Era'* brickmaking machinery were still using their distinctive telegraphic address *'Bricks'* and were proud to say that they had been in business over a hundred years. The family took the business into liquidation in 1972.

ESTABLISHED 1854.

Telephone: **32755** ACCRINGTON.

Telegraphic Address:
"BRICKS, ACCRINGTON."

Reference { OURS ___ { YOURS ___

C. WHITTAKER & Co. Ld,

DOWRY STREET IRONWORKS,

ACCRINGTON,
ENGLAND.

Bert Johnson captured t' Stanley's Peel Park ground in 1967. We see the Coppice beyond, from which he took the other photograph about 1964. In 1962, former Grammar School teacher Ronnie Digby penned the poem on the next page about the hill given to the town in 1907 by the Peel family.

# Th'Coppice

Tha must be cowd i't'winter
Thi grassy cooat's thin
It's nooan as green neaw neither
As whod id wer long sin':
An th'air tha breathes is smooky,
Tha'rt noan so far fro' t'teawn.
An' when it rains day after day
Tha seems to weear a freawn.
Tha'rt nooan as big as Pendle yon,
Tha doesn't reych to t'stars,
Tha's no songs sung abeawt thi
An' on thi face tha's scars;
Bud then, tha's music o'thi own,
Tha's no need to despair,
Th'owd wind comes whistlin' oe'r thi
An' larks sing up in th'air.
An'then Ah've sin thi smilin'
When t'sky's aw blue aboon,
Or when tha'rt watchin' t'cooarters
Bi' t'gentle leet o't'moon.
As eawt be, tha'rt nooan lonely
When aw is said an'done.
Aw t'childer come to see thi'
Fro'deawn i'Accrington.
Tha'rt bonny too, owd Coppy,
When t'thorns are white i'May,
An' when tha blushes pink, as t'sun
Gets low near th'end o't'day.
An'when tha bears, i' Holy Week
Upon thi top, a cross,
An meks fooak think o'Calvary,
Fer words Ah'm at a loss.

The town's freemasons joined in the coronation celebrations in 1911. This was but one of several processions held that day. The weather was *'blustery and threatening with some rain in early morning'*.

A carnival day procession approaches Church just before 1930,when *'Ribble Motors'*, with a financial stake from the Corporation, bought the Antley Bus Company's garage. Accrington *'fire bobbies'* are passing the garage and the *'Antley Inn'* with the Methodist chapel in the far distance. Can you hear the skirl of the pipes and the beating of the drums as children thrill at seeing the Pipe Major throw his mace into the air, never failing to catch it? *(Alan Parkin Collection)*

Two successive pictures taken by an unknown photographer whose distinctive handwriting adorns many picture postcards of that era. The New Jerusalem elders and scholars pass the *'Imperial Hotel'* at the top of King Street on their way to the stone-laying ceremony at St Andrew's church in 1912. These, and a photograph on the opposite page, were taken from a vantage point near *'Kendalls' Temperance Hotel'* at the junction of Blackburn Road and Fox Street.

---O---

### Parkin.

10oz. meal, 12oz. flour, 8oz. sugar, 8oz. butter, 4oz. treacle, pinch of salt, 1 teaspoonful of ginger, small teaspoonful of carbonate of soda.

*Method*—Mix dry ingredients together; melt butter and treacle, mix thoroughly, and add sufficient milk to make a stiff paste; bake in a slow oven for 45 minutes.

MRS. TIPPING, 192, Blackburn Road, Accrington.

---O---

It is unusual for those who submit recipes for publication to have their address as well as their name shown. It is not suggested that Mrs Tipping sought to use this to advantage, but readers may wish to know that Mrs Tipping's husband ran a grocery shop near to the Grammar School selling the ingredients for parkin (Not from the Alan Parkin Collection).

61

Roses don't like too much rain, and certainly this *'Rose Queen'* wouldn't either, but she got it on Saturday 13th July 1907. It was the sixth Rose Queen Festival organised by St James' church and Sunday school. Young Belle Calvert was attended by twelve maids of honour, and followed from Waterloo Street to the sports field at Dunkenhalgh Park by a procession which included 24 maypole dancers, 24 morris dancers, 24 *'gypsies'* from St James' and 24 sailor boys. Some photographs of the event show a John Bull character. He was William McQuilton from Helmshore and is seen on photographs taken all over Lancashire in this period.

On one of these photographs can be seen a man who called himself *'the clerk of the weather'*. He carried a sign saying *'Have you seen Summer?'* What do you think the bystanders said to him? The *'Accrington Observer'* contained a line reading *'the beautifully decorated lurries were soaked beyond redemption'*. How very true.

ROSE CARNIVAL. II

Themed bazaars were an important means of fund-raising for churches. This is the committee set up to organise a *'Grand Bazaar'* for the Clayton Baptist church and Sunday school in the Mechanics' Institute over four days in December 1910. Rev Ishmael Jones, the pastor is seen leaning on the pedestal. Here too we see the admission prices. Thanks to the generosity of William Haworth (£100) and Sir George Macalpine (£250), £540 was raised on the first day, a Wednesday. On this page you will read a recipe, probably written by Accrington author Richard Ainsworth, who captured the humour often found within bazaar handbooks.

" *Rare noteworthy object.*"—*Two Gentlemen of Verona.*

## Object of the Bazaar.

## £1,000 OR MORE.

For the purpose of Building a New Sunday School, which will cost at least £2,500.

*Thus have you heard our cause.*—*Henry IV.*

## Prices of Admission.

| | | |
|---|---|---|
| Family Season Tickets | - - | 5/- |
| Single Season Tickets | - - | 2/- |
| First Day | - - - - | 1/6 |
| .. after 6 o'clock | - - | 1/- |
| Second Day | - - - - | 1/- |
| Third Day (Children's) | - - | 6d. |
| Fourth Day | - - - - | 6d. |

*Children under 12, Half-price.*

Tickets may be had from the Stallholders and Committee, and at the Door.

CLUB TICKETS may be used for any purpose except Admission.

" *It is a pleasing figure,*
*But methinks it is fixed too low.*"

─────o─────

## A Good Bazaar Worker.

Take of goodness, generosity, and commonsense each a goodly portion ; add industry, perseverance, and skill with good taste, and the capacity for picking other people's pockets. Flavour with patience and good temper. Thoroughly mix with the milk of human kindness.

R. AINSWORTH.

Mr Constantine published this postcard, but probably didn't take the photograph. It was printed in Germany, as were most of the earliest postcards, and says on the back *'This part may be used for correspondence'*. This reminded purchasers that the Post Office now (from 1904) allowed a message as well as an address to be written on the back. The couple are standing at the corner of Plantation Street and what was then called Cobham Street. It became *'Road'* later.

Pursuing his hobby of capturing bits of Accrington which are about to fall to the bulldozer, Bert Johnson's view of the *'New Hippodrome'* was blocked by a Corporation 'bus from the Ellison Street depot next door. Built in double-quick time in 1908 to replace one burnt down, demolition took place in 1972.

Elephant Street ran between Birtwistle Street and Plantation Street. The properties were put up in 1845 when a 5-ton elephant, worth £800, belonging to a visiting circus dropped dead in the town. Urban myth has it that the animal, *'Chimey'*, was buried under the then un-named street's setts. Bert Johnson captured the view down from Plantation Street, with the former *'Welcome Inn'* painted white, before the demolition men came in 1972.

Mrs Pomfret was probably the organiser of the morris team who danced in the 1910 Co-op Jubilee procession. Here we behold her and her charges, with not a few mothers and dads, on the steps of the Conservative Club in Cannon Street. How many are without a hat? When opened in October 1891, the club was the largest such club in the country. It was paid for with the generosity of John Bullough. The architecture was 'Queen Anne' style.

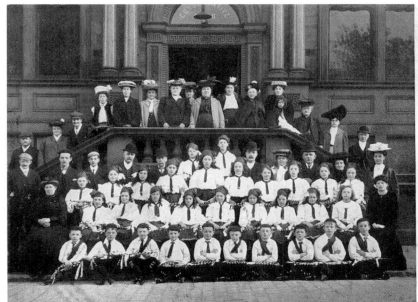

Mrs. POMFRET,

*Organizer.*

&

The Morris Dancers of the Accrington Provident Co-operative Society, Ltd. Head Offices : 4 Stanley Street.

*Photos. by A. Greenwood*

This photograph was sent to Mrs Arthur Hodgson in Clement Street in 1906 and is likely a family group. It serves to show us the fashion of the Edwardian era, and points out that deck chair cloth designs have not altered much since then. There were two Hodgson households in Clement Street.

'*Scatclyff*' was mentioned in legal papers as early as 1542. This area of the town gave its name to the coal mine opened up in 1859 and which eventually had a shaft 550 feet deep. It closed in 1962. This photograph was taken after 1948 when the pit, one several operated by the Hargreaves family, was nationalised under the '*N.C.B. -National Coal Board*' banner.

Not too long before closure, these photographs were taken on the '*pit top*'. (*Photos – Frank Watson Collection*)

Peel Mill was also known as *'Milnshaw Mill'*. It was in Lupin Road and was built in 1905 by the *'Accrington Mill Building Company'*, which was set up to provide buildings which manufacturers could lease. Before this, Accrington had one loom to every three residents, whereas Nelson had 1-to-1 and Blackburn 1–to-2. The local Co-op society was behind this enterprise, which was chaired by Thomas Whittaker of the Dowry Street engineering company, which built the mill's engine. The Co-op put up a £15,000 mortgage in support. The Weavers' Association bought shares at £1,000 and Whittakers £1,200. There were 500 employees by 1920. The mill was sold in 1959 to Burco Dean of Burnley. Their subsidiaries, *'H.Slack & Co'* and *'Pannette Holloware'* also moved in. How many styles of hat were there in fashion in 1913 when these chaps (there's no females aboard) went on this trip? They would surely need more than one *'sharra'*, which the older chaps would call a *'charabanc'*.

23rd June 1920 was a Wednesday. The town had almost come to a standstill, for its tradesmen were all, or most of 'em, away for the day. They went to many locations – the grocers to Wharfedale, the chemists to Windermere, this lot to Blackpool where one of the town's *'smudgers'* caught them and would have the photographs back by the time they departed. The *'Accrington Observer'* reported…*'Accrington had not nearly sufficient charries to supply the demand and motor vehicles were engaged from a number of local town'*.

The *'holiday trek'* scene on the railway station was reported upon in a (Tuesday) July edition of the *'Accrington Observer'* about 1920. The photographer was Mr Carr, about whom nothing is known. In later years the same scene would be snapped by the ubiquitous cameraman Garth Dawson.

Hillock Farm stood on the Huncoat side of the Coppice slopes. Its land was bought around 1910 to complement that given to the town by the Peels, turning the whole of the Coppice, previously known as *'John Hoyle's Coppice'* after an occupier of Hillock Farm, which was of the Tudor period. This photograph was taken by Mr Stott, a professional photographer based in Nelson and Accrington. It was probably taken in the 1920s. Writing in 1928, Richard Ainsworth, author of *'The Old Homesteads of Accrington & District'* expressed the wish that it would never have to suffer demolition and would be restored to something like its original state. He knew that the Corporation owned it. Wishful thinking?

Mr Stott caught these workmen at Slate Pits farm on a sunny day. The farmhouse was (is, for it still stands) not grand yet it was strong and sturdy, being framed with oak trees and roofed with one-inch thick slabs of stone dug from the ground nearby, whence came the stone for its exterior. Moleside provided it with shelter from stormy blasts. The ancient *'King's Highway'* was nearby to connect this, and other outlying farms, to the outside world. Now, access is via Plantation Street and under the motorway.

This is a 1910 postcard which serves as greetings and advertisement, for on the back is written *'Greetings from your milkman, Abraham Matthews, Higher Fir Trees Farm, Altham'*. His cart was known as a *'float'* and the milk was carried in *'kits'* before being poured into the customers' jugs left on doorsteps.

Accrington bricks are world famous, but many of them were made in Huncoat, which only became part of the borough in 1928. One such was known as a *'Redac'* (i.e. a red Accrington brick), no doubt equal in quality to a *'Nori'*. The former was made in this brickworks, the latter in the Whinney Hill one, seen over to the far left. The material used for them was called *'shale'* rather than *'clay'*. Huncoat brickworks was fed from the Burnley Road quarry by an aerial runway. It was dismantled in the 1960s, and the works closed at the end of 1992. A *'Nori'* became a noun in its own right, just as an electric vacuum cleaner became known as a *'hoover'*. Evidence of this is found in the phrase *"Ah chucked 'afe a nori at 'im"*. *(Photo- John Goddard Collection)*

These *'good men and true'* were the committee of the Huncoat Baptist chapel in the early years of the century. Some of their family names are still to be found in this village which continues to see itself as separate to Accrington.
*Back Row*: John Lock, Peter Yeoman, Dick Bank, James Ridehalgh, Jim Astwell
*Middle*: John Haworth, Joseph Jaques, Dick Greenwood, John Cunliffe, John Whittaker
*Front*: Robert Suthers, Rushton Cunliffe, William Haworth

Town Clerk Aitken, after whom Aitken Street is named, walks with Mayor Thomas Edward Higham (later knighted) from Daisy Hill into Christ Church Street in either 1906 or 1907, for he was mayor two years in succession.

This is Christ Church Square, through which Mayor Higham walked on his way to the church. Today, it is Accrington's only 'square'. *(Photo-June Huntingdon)*

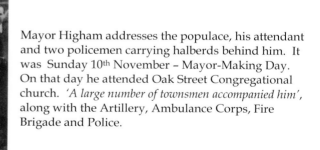

Mayor Higham addresses the populace, his attendant and two policemen carrying halberds behind him. It was Sunday 10th November – Mayor-Making Day. On that day he attended Oak Street Congregational church. *'A large number of townsmen accompanied him'*, along with the Artillery, Ambulance Corps, Fire Brigade and Police.

On the left we see Thomas Boyd, the Parks Superintendent, and on the opposite side of a beautiful display of October-flowering chrysanthemums are Charles Williamson, chairman of the Corporation's Parks Committee and Henry Parkinson. The location is the *'Henry Parkinson Greenhouse'*. Henry was perhaps the most generous benefactor the town has ever had. He gave to Oak Hill Park and the grammar school, styling himself *'Accrington Friend and Wellwisher'*. He founded the forerunner of today's Hyndburn Local History Society and sponsored the writer Richard Ainsworth to chronicle history. He died in 1938, a year after the photograph was taken. If ever a chap deserved a knighthood, it was Henry Parkinson. *(Photo – Accrington Local Studies Library)*

Was Henry Parkinson, seen in the photograph, the model for this *'Gas & Water Board'* advert?

There was water a-plenty in this place – the Corporation's Public Baths in St James Street at its junction with Paradise Street, which is just seen on the right. Out of sight at this point on the right stands, or possibly stood by March 1977 when the photograph was taken, the *'Junction Inn'*, much frequented by those attending the dances at the nearby Conservative Club. The sixteen *'slipper'* baths and the swimming bath were opened in 1911. They cost a total of £10,132 and were designed by Mr Newton, the borough architect. What was referred to in the Corporation's 1928 Jubilee book as the swimming *'pond'* measured 75 feet by 30, and increased in depth from 3ft 6inches to 6ft 9inches. Can you smell the chlorine?

There is much to be learned from old newspapers. Here are two examples, one giving us a hint of how our streets came to be lit by gas at a very early time, and another telling of the demise of a much-loved but uneconomic form of transport in March 1932. Seen with it is an advert from a 1956 *'Accrington Observer'*. The *'Accrington Permanent Building Society'* had been formed in 1875 and amalgamated with the larger *'Cheshire Building Society'* in 1982.

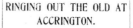

**RINGING OUT THE OLD AT ACCRINGTON.**

---

**LAST TRAM REACHES JOURNEY'S END.**

The undertakings of tramway service in Accrington comes to an end shortly before midnight to-night, when the last car, the 11 p.m. from Blackburn to Accrington centre, makes its final trip. Some of the trams, which several years ago cost something like £2,000, can now be obtained for £25. For a country residence, a summer-house, or sports pavilion, a tram body is now available at £20 for a single-decker, £10 for the bottom deck of a double-decker, and £5 for the top deck.

Other Corporation departments have bought several for various uses, a number being utilised for sports accommodation in playing fields and parks. At one time the Corporation possessed 38 cars, and now about 26 are for sale.

The district's first tram tracks were laid in 1884, 1885, 1886 between Accrington and Church, and between Baxenden and Clayton le-Moors. They were leased to Accrington Corporation Steam Tramways Company for 21 years. The official opening took place on April 8, 1886, when three steam-trams were put into commission. These cars had carried by the end of April 37,370 passengers.

GET OUT AND PUSH.

Many humorous stories have been told about the old steam trams. On the hilly routes, it is said, many times passengers had to get out and push.

In 1905 the Corporation promoted a bill which gave them authority to work the tramways to electric power, and also to extend the service to Oswaldtwistle and Huncoat. On August 7, 1907, the first electric tram ran on the Accrington to Church route, on which the last car finishes to-night.

The through running of trams-between Accrington and Blackburn has been in operation since August, 1907. To meet the demands of modern transport requirements the Corporation decided to start bus services, the first route to be opened being Huncoat in November, 1928. Since then, as the tramway tracks have been pulled up, buses superseded the electric cars, and to-day 48 buses are in operation on various routes, with only one tram, which is plying between Accrington and Blackburn.

Bert Johnson looked down from the Coppice in the 1970s. In the distance, this side of the 21 arches of the railway viaduct, he could see Union Street Methodist chapel and not a few chimneys. That he could see so far was perhaps thanks to the newly-introduced *'smokeless fuel'* measures to promote cleaner air.